SAND

by
Ellen J. Prager

illustrated by
Nancy Woodman

▢ NATIONAL GEOGRAPHIC SOCIETY
Washington, D.C.

To

all those who have inspired

my love of the sea

and allowed me to

walk, swim, and dive

within its sandy, wondrous realm.

E.J.P.

To

all who see the world

in a grain of sand.

N.W.

Beaches are made of sand.

Desert dunes are made of sand.

Sand can be home to crabs and clams or seagulls and stingrays. People like to walk on sand, lie on sand, and build big sandcastles.

What is sand?
Where does sand come from?
And how does sand get to the ocean's edge
on a beach or piled high into a tall sand dune?
Let the sand sleuth show you the way!

5

We use the word SAND to describe the size of a grain.

Sand is made up of grains smaller than gravel but bigger than mud in size.

Gravel

Sand

Mud

Sand grains often come from rocks that have been broken down into smaller and smaller pieces over a very long period of time. Sand can also be made of small pieces of crystal, shell, lava, or coral.

Red Sand

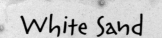

White Sand

Green Sand

Sand can be many colors—white, red, green, tan, or black. Some sand even looks like the black and white of a Dalmatian's spotted coat.

Tan Sand

Black Sand

Black-and-
White Sand

The color of sand comes from the color of its grains.

Sand made from coral and shells forms the whitest of white beaches.

Waves crashing onto a coral reef bring bits and chunks of coral and shells to the beach and, over time, create sparkling white beaches along tropical shores.

Sometimes sand is made of crystals.
Crystals are made of minerals, and minerals come
from rocks. Crystals of different minerals form
sands of different colors.

Green sand is commonly made up of
small crystals of the mineral olivine.

Crystals of the mineral garnet can make sand look red.

One of the most common minerals found on land is quartz. Quartz crystals can be many colors—pink, gray, brown, white, or clear—and usually make sand look tan or off-white.

Many sands are made up of a mixture of grain types, including rock fragments, mineral crystals, and shell or coral pieces.

This spotted sand is made up of white coral pieces and black rock fragments.

This colorful sand is a mix of red rock fragments and green crystals.

Quartz crystals and rock fragments make this sand look gray.

When a volcano erupts, hot molten rock, called lava, can flow down to the sea. Where hot lava and cool ocean meet, towers of steam rise high into the sky.

Cool water turns the fiery red lava into hard black rock. Very quick cooling can cause the rock to shatter into small, shiny black pieces—instant black sand.

Now you know what sand looks like up close and what it is commonly made of.
But how does sand get onto a beach or built into a tall sand dune?

There are several different ways that sand can be moved from one place to another.

Water

Wind

Ice

Rivers can carry rocks from high in the mountains to faraway seashores.

Wind can pick up sand grains and create small ripples, like tiny waves on water, or build sand dunes as tall as buildings.

Sand grains that have been blown by the wind tend to have pointy sides and look frosted.

As rocks are washed down toward the sea, they bump against each other, breaking down into smaller and smaller pieces—creating sand.

Ocean waves and currents can move sand from one beach to another or carry sand from the floor of the sea onto the beach. During a storm big waves can move sand or gravel onto a beach or take it away.

Sand grains on beaches that are pounded by big waves become round and shiny by bumping and rubbing against each other in the water.

Ice can trap sand in its chilly grip and carry it to the sea. When the ice melts, the sand falls onto the land or into the water.

Sand, Sand, Sand

It comes in many colors but only
a few sizes. Remember, sand is
just a grain size: bigger than
mud but smaller than gravel.
If you look close, you might
see pieces of coral, shells,
or crystals in the sand.
Flowing water, blowing
wind, or moving ice
can break big rocks into
small pieces and bring
them to a beach where
wind can build tall dunes.

Next time you walk on a sandy beach, climb a high sand dune, or get ready to build a big sandcastle, bend down and scoop up a handful of sand.

What is it made of? How did it get there? Look for clues hidden in the grains to answer your questions!

SHAKE IT UP!

If you'd like to try and make some sand on your own, here's what you'll need....

An empty coffee can with a lid
A cup of clean water
3 or 4 small rocks (pebbles)
A clear plastic cup
A magnifier (optional)

1) Before starting the experiment, rinse out the coffee can and clean off the rocks so that there's no loose dirt on them.

2) Place the rocks in the can and add the cup of water. Snap the lid on tight and get ready to shake, rattle, and roll!

3) Holding the can so that the lid is on top, shake the can with the rocks and water as hard as you can for about three minutes.
If you get tired, take a break and start again. You may even want to put on your favorite song to dance to while you're shaking.

4) After three minutes of shaking, carefully remove the lid from the can and pour some of the water into the clear plastic cup. How does the water look now? Why is it cloudy instead of clear? (Tiny pieces of rock broke off to make the water look dirty).

5) Take out the rocks and look at them closely. How have they changed?

6) Run your finger along the bottom of the can. Do you feel something rough and gritty? Look at the grit with a magnifier. Can you guess what you've made? SAND!

By shaking the can with the water and the rocks, you were just like the current in a river or the waves in the ocean. The moving water made the rocks hit together. Little by little small pieces chipped off to make sand. The longer you shake, the more sand you make!

If you want to make more sand, try using different types of rocks to see how the sand changes. You can even experiment by using some small pieces of shell or coral.

Published by the
National Geographic Society
1145 17th Street N.W.
Washington, D.C. 20036

The artwork in this book is a digital collage of pastels on sandpaper,
watercolors, and photographs. The photographs shown through the
sandpiper sleuth's magnifying glass were taken through a microscope.

Book design by Nancy Woodman

Library of Congress Cataloging-in-Publication Data
Prager, Ellen J.
Sand / by Ellen J. Prager
p. cm.
Summary: Describes the formation of sand from materials such as
coral, rock, or crystals and shows how it can be moved through
water, wind, ice, and other erosion agents.
ISBN 0-7922-7104-1
[1. Sand-Juvenile Literature.] I. Woodman, Nancy, ill. II. Title.
QE471.2.P7   2000
553.6'22—dc21   99-29943

PHOTOGRAPHY CREDITS: Cover, back cover center — Robert Dashiell;
back cover right and left — David Gaddis; pp.1,2,3,28,29,32 — Nancy Woodman;
pp. 8,9,12,13,14,15 — Mark Thiessen, NGP; pp.11,12,13,14,15,16,23,24 (close-ups) — Ellen J. Prager

Experiment written by Stephen M. Tomecek

Printed in Mexico

The world's largest nonprofit scientific and educational organization, the National Geographic Society was founded in 1888 "for the increase and diffusion of geographic knowledge."
Since then it has supported scientific exploration and spread information to its more than nine million members worldwide.
The National Geographic Society educates and inspires millions every day through magazines, books, television programs, videos, maps and atlases, research grants,
the National Geography Bee, teacher workshops, and innovative classroom materials. The Society is supported through membership dues and income from the sale of its educational products.
Members receive NATIONAL GEOGRAPHIC magazine—the Society's official journal—discounts on Society products, and other benefits.
For more information about the National Geographic Society and its educational programs and publications, please call 1-800-NGS-LINE (647-5463), or write to the following address:
National Geographic Society
1145 17th Street N.W.
Washington, D.C. 20036-4688 U.S.A.
Visit the Society's Web site: www.nationalgeographic.com

PUEBLO

Big Buddy Books
An Imprint of Abdo Publishing
abdopublishing.com

Katie Lajiness

abdopublishing.com

Published by Abdo Publishing, a division of ABDO, PO Box 398166, Minneapolis, Minnesota 55439.
Copyright © 2017 by Abdo Consulting Group, Inc. International copyrights reserved in all countries. No part
of this book may be reproduced in any form without written permission from the publisher. Big Buddy Books™
is a trademark and logo of Abdo Publishing.

Printed in the United States of America, North Mankato, Minnesota.
062016
092016

THIS BOOK CONTAINS
RECYCLED MATERIALS

Cover Photo: © NativeStock.com/AngelWynn; Shutterstock.com.
Interior Photos: ASSOCIATED PRESS (pp. 5, 25); © Bettmann/Corbis (p. 15); © George H.H. Huey/Corbis
    (pp. 16, 17); © iStockphoto.com (pp. 11, 17, 26); © W. Langdon Kihn/National Geographic Creative/Corbis
    (p. 23); © NativeStock.com/AngelWynn (pp. 9, 13, 17); © Joel Rogers/Corbis (p. 21); Shutterstock.com
    (pp. 26, 27, 29, 30); © Marilyn Angel Wynn/Nativestock Pictures/Corbis (p. 19).

Quote on page 30 from the National Park Service.

Coordinating Series Editor: Tamara L. Britton
Graphic Design: Adam Craven

Library of Congress Cataloging-in-Publication Data

Lajiness, Katie, author.
   Pueblo / Katie Lajiness.
Minneapolis, MN : ABDO Publishing Company, 2017. | Series:
   Native Americans
LCCN 2015050494| ISBN 9781680782011 | ISBN 9781680774962 (ebook)
Pueblo Indians--History--Juvenile literature. | Pueblo
   Indians--Social life and customs--Juvenile literature.
LCC E99.P9 L3214 2017 | DDC 978.9004/974--dc23
LC record available at http://lccn.loc.gov/2015050494

CONTENTS

Amazing People

Hundreds of years ago, North America was mostly wild, open land. Native American tribes lived on the land. They had their own languages and **customs**.

The Pueblo (PWEH-bloh) are one Native American tribe. They are known for their **adobe** houses and beautiful pottery. Let's learn more about these Native Americans.

Did You Know?

The name *Pueblo* means "village" or "town" in Spanish.

Pueblo children honor their history and traditions at festivals.

5

PUEBLO TERRITORY

Pueblo homelands were mostly in the American Southwest. Most tribes lived in what is now Arizona, Colorado, New Mexico, and Utah. They established villages along the Rio Grande River.

The Pueblo come from the Anasazi (ah-nuh-SAH-zee) people who lived about 7,000 years ago. Today there are 21 tribes. Each speaks one of six languages.

Did You Know?

From the Pueblo tribes, the Hopi still live in Arizona. And, the Acoma, Laguna, and Zuni people live in New Mexico.

CANADA

UNITED STATES

MEXICO

PUEBLO HOMELANDS

UTAH

COLORADO

ARIZONA

NEW MEXICO

N
W E
S

HOME LIFE

Many Pueblo families lived in villages on top of **mesas**. The Pueblo built homes with **adobe** and stone. The homes had many levels. Some had more than 100 rooms!

The Pueblo also built **kivas** for **ceremonies**. People used ladders to climb down into them.

Today, an ancient mission built over a Pueblo village still stands. It is open to the public at the Pecos National Historical Park in New Mexico.

9

What They Ate

The Pueblo were skilled farmers. They grew corn, beans, and squash. Their land was very dry, so women collected water to wet the soil.

Depending on where they lived, Pueblo men hunted different animals. They hunted antelope, bison, deer, or rabbits.

Corn was a common crop in a Pueblo village. They dried and stored it to eat later.

DAILY LIFE

Each village had its own government, but the Pueblo tribes shared similar **customs**. They had strong ties to their **traditions** and homeland.

The Pueblo wore few clothes. Men wore **loincloths**. Women wore dresses called *mantas*. Everyone wore moccasins made from deer hide.

The Pueblo wore traditional headdresses during special ceremonies. And, women often carried pottery on top of their heads.

13

In a Pueblo village, people had different tasks. Men farmed plants and hunted animals. And, they built **adobe** homes. Women took care of the children and the home. They also gathered and made food.

Children learned by helping and watching adults. Girls made baskets and pottery with their mothers and grandmothers. Boys learned to make bows and arrows from their fathers and grandfathers.

Some men hunted on horseback. This way, it was easier to carry animals back to the village.

MADE BY HAND

The Pueblo made many objects by hand. They often used natural materials. These arts and crafts added beauty to everyday life.

Pottery
Pueblo women were famous for making clay pots by hand. The pots were decorated with designs of shapes, animals, or flowers.

Adobe Brick Ovens

The Pueblo baked bread in adobe ovens. These ovens stayed hot long after the fire died.

Jewelry

The Pueblo traded their goods for items such as seashells. Then the women turned seashells into jewelry.

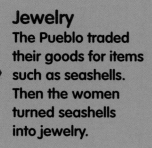

Hunting Tools

Around 1100 AD, the Anasazi made axes. They used willow to tie the stone to the wooden handle.

Sandals

The Pueblo used yucca plants to make sandals.

SPIRIT LIFE

The Pueblo believed every object had a spirit.
The people thought the spirits brought rain for
crops and animals for hunting. So, they held
ceremonies to keep the spirits happy.

Kachinas were Pueblo spirits. Pueblo men held
kachina dances to honor the spirits of the earth,
sky, and water. They wore masks to look like
these spirits.

During ceremonies, native dancers wore clothes decorated with feathers and beads. They shook rattles to the beat.

19

STORYTELLERS

Stories are important to the Pueblo. They shared tales about their native **culture** and history.

The Pueblo's stories explain their beliefs, songs, and dances. Their tales keep the Pueblo's **customs** alive.

Cave drawings were one way the ancient Pueblos shared stories. Drawings found in Utah tell stories about hunting on horseback.

FIGHTING FOR LAND

From 1276 to 1299, the Pueblo battled over land with nearby tribes. So, many Pueblo moved to what is now Arizona and New Mexico.

In 1598, the Spanish built a settlement near a Pueblo village. They ordered the Native Americans to share crops. And, many were pushed to become **Catholics**.

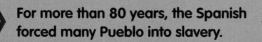

For more than 80 years, the Spanish forced many Pueblo into slavery.

23

In 1680, a medicine man name Popé (poh-PAY) led a successful fight against the Spanish. The Pueblo lived peacefully until the Spanish returned in 1691. Again, the Pueblo fought to protect their territory.

From 1821 to 1846, Mexico ruled the Pueblo's lands. In 1848, the United States took control of the area. The government forced the Pueblo to practice American **customs** and learn English.

Popé was a spiritual leader. He wanted the Pueblo to defeat the Spanish and return to their traditional lifestyle.

BACK IN TIME

700

The Anasazi made special pottery decorated with black-and-white designs. The pots were used for **ceremonies** and trade.

100

The Pueblo combined hunting and gathering food with farming corn.

1100s

The Pueblo lived in large communities. Many homes were built into canyons. People entered their homes by climbing a ladder.

1300s

For many years, a lack of rain made the Pueblo's land very dry. They struggled to farm the land and grow crops. Many left their villages and moved to find water.

1970

The US government returned Blue Lake along with about 48,000 acres (19,000 ha) to the Taos Pueblo of New Mexico.

1500s

Spanish settlers and **missionaries** came to New Mexico. The Pueblo were not used to European sicknesses. So, many Native Americans died.

THE PUEBLO TODAY

The Pueblo have a long, rich history. They are remembered for their beautiful crafts and **ceremonies**.

Pueblo roots run deep. Today, the people have kept alive those special things that make them Pueblo. Even though times have changed, many people carry the **traditions**, stories, and memories of the past into the present.

Did You Know?

Today, there are about 50,000 Pueblo living in the United States.

The Pueblo have lived in the same area longer than any other people in North America. Taos, New Mexico, has been their home for more than 700 years!

"Through oral **traditions** and dances we know that the spirits of our ancestors are still present in our homes on the plateau."

– Gary Roybal,
San Ildefonso Pueblo

GLOSSARY

adobe (uh-DOH-bee) a type of brick or building material made from sun-dried earth and straw.

Catholic a member of the Roman Catholic Church. This kind of Christianity has been around since the first century and is led by the pope.

ceremony a formal event on a special occasion.

culture (KUHL-chuhr) the arts, beliefs, and ways of life of a group of people.

custom a practice that has been around a long time and is common to a group or a place.

kiva (KEE-vuh) a Pueblo ceremonial structure that is usually round and partly underground.

loincloth a simple cloth worn by a man to cover his lower body.

mesa (MAY-suh) a hill with a flat top and steep sides.

missionary a person who travels to share his or her religious beliefs with others. A mission is a place where religious work is done.

tradition (truh-DIH-shuhn) a belief, a custom, or a story handed down from older people to younger people.

WEBSITES

To learn more about Native Americans, visit **booklinks.abdopublishing.com**. These links are routinely monitored and updated to provide the most current information available.

INDEX